NIGEL PLANER

Nigel Planer has written several b[...] *The Right Man* and *Faking It* (pu[...] as the best-selling *A Good Enough Dad* and the spoof theatrical biography *I, An Actor*, (Methuen; with Christopher Douglas) which also spawned two BBC TV series, a radio series and a one-man theatre show as Nicholas Craig.

After appearing at the Birmingham Writers' Festival in 1996, he toured the country as a performance poet and published a short collection of poetry called *Unlike the Buddha* (Jackson's Arm) as well as regularly contributing to the Guardian poetry spot in the 1990s. With his brother Roger he scripted and voiced more than one hundred episodes of *The Magic Roundabout* for Channel 4.

After training at LAMDA, Nigel Planer co-founded London's Comedy Store and Comic Strip clubs and went on to star in the classic television series *The Young Ones* and *The Comic Strip Presents*. He has appeared in leading roles in countless TV programmes, both comic and dramatic, including the long-running *Shine on Harvey Moon*, *The Grimleys*, Michael Palin's *Number 27*, Simon Gray's *Two Lumps of Ice* and *Frankenstein's Baby* by Emma Tennant. Film appearances include *Land Girls*, *Brazil*, Stephen Fry's *Bright Young Things* and *The Decameron*. He has also appeared, mostly in new plays, at the Bush, the Lyric, the Traverse, the Young Vic, West Yorkshire Playhouse, Plymouth Drum and Hampstead Theatre.

He starred in the original London casts of *Evita*, *Chicago* and *We Will Rock You*, the smash-hit political satire *Feelgood*, and Ayckbourn's *Man of the Moment* where he took over the lead role from Michael Gambon.

In the guise of Neil the hippy, Nigel has twice topped the British pop charts, gaining silver and gold discs and winning a Brit award in 1985. As part of the spoof Heavy Metal band Bad News, he made two albums produced by Brian May and played the Hammersmith Apollo and Donington and Reading Rock Festivals.

On the Ceiling is his first play.

Other Titles in this Series

Simon Block
CHIMPS
HAND IN HAND
NOT A GAME FOR BOYS
A PLACE AT THE TABLE

Caryl Churchill
BLUE HEART
CHURCHILL PLAYS: THREE
CHURCHILL: SHORTS
CLOUD NINE
A DREAM PLAY
  after Strindberg
FAR AWAY
HOTEL
ICECREAM
LIGHT SHINING IN
  BUCKINGHAMSHIRE
MAD FOREST
A NUMBER
THE SKRIKER
THIS IS A CHAIR
THYESTES *after* Seneca
TRAPS

Helen Edmundson
ANNA KARENINA
  after Tolstoy
THE CLEARING
GONE TO EARTH *after* Webb
THE MILL ON THE FLOSS
  after Eliot
MOTHER TERESA IS DEAD
WAR AND PEACE *after* Tolstoy

Kevin Elyot
THE DAY I STOOD STILL
ELYOT: FOUR PLAYS
FORTY WINKS
MOUTH TO MOUTH
MY NIGHT WITH REG

Stephen Jeffreys
THE CLINK
A GOING CONCERN
I JUST STOPPED BY TO SEE
  THE MAN
THE LIBERTINE

Marie Jones
STONES IN HIS POCKETS
  & A NIGHT IN NOVEMBER

Edward Kemp
5/11
NATHAN THE WISE
  after Lessing

Ayub Khan-Din
EAST IS EAST
LAST DANCE AT DUM-DUM
NOTES ON FALLING LEAVES

Tony Kushner
ANGELS IN AMERICA
  PARTS ONE & TWO
HOMEBODY/KABUL

Owen McCafferty
CLOSING TIME
DAYS OF WINE AND ROSES
  after JP Miller
MOJO MICKYBO
SCENES FROM THE BIG
  PICTURE
SHOOT THE CROW

Conor McPherson
DUBLIN CAROL
McPHERSON: FOUR PLAYS
McPHERSON PLAYS: TWO
PORT AUTHORITY
SHINING CITY
THE WEIR

Arthur Miller
AN ENEMY OF THE PEOPLE
  after Ibsen
PLAYING FOR TIME

Jack Shepherd
THROUGH A CLOUD

Imogen Stubbs
WE HAPPY FEW

Enda Walsh
BEDBOUND & MISTERMAN
DISCO PIGS
  & SUCKING DUBLIN
THE SMALL THINGS

Nicholas Wright
CRESSIDA
HIS DARK MATERIALS
  after Pullman
MRS KLEIN
VINCENT IN BRIXTON
WRIGHT: FIVE PLAYS

Nigel Planer

ON THE CEILING

NICK HERN BOOKS

LONDON

www.nickhernbooks.co.uk

A Nick Hern Book

On the Ceiling first published in Great Britain as a paperback original in 2005 by Nick Hern Books Limited, 14 Larden Road, London W3 7ST

On the Ceiling copyright © 2005 Nigel Planer

Nigel Planer has asserted his right to be identified as the author of this work

Cover Image: photography by Hugo Glendinning; design by SWD

Typeset by Country Setting, Kingsdown, Kent, CT14 8ES
Printed in Great Britain by Cox and Wyman, Reading, Berks

A CIP catalogue record for this book is available from the British Library

ISBN-13   978 1 85459 902 5
ISBN-10   1 85459 902 X

CAUTION   All rights whatsoever in this play are strictly reserved. Requests to reproduce the text in whole or in part should be addressed to the publisher.

Amateur Performing Rights   Applications for performance, including readings and excerpts, by amateurs in English should be addressed to the Performing Rights Manager, Nick Hern Books, 14 Larden Road, London W3 7ST, *fax* +44 (0)20 8735 0250 *e-mail* info@nickhernbooks.demon.co.uk, except as follows:

Australia: Dominie Drama, 8 Cross Street, Brookvale 2100, *fax* (2) 9905 5209, *e-mail* dominie@dominie.com.au

New Zealand: Play Bureau, PO Box 420, New Plymouth, *fax* (6) 753 2150, *e-mail* play.bureau.nz@xtra.co.nz

United States of America and Canada: Peters Fraser & Dunlop, see details below

Professional Performing Rights   Applications for performance by professionals in any medium and in any language throughout the world should be addressed to Peters Fraser & Dunlop, Drury House, 34-43 Russell Street, London WC2B 5HA, *fax* +44 (0)20 7836 9541

No performance of any kind may be given unless a licence has been obtained. Applications should be made before rehearsals begin. Publication of this play does not necessarily indicate its availability for performance.

On the Ceiling was first performed at Birmingham Repertory Theatre, by arrangement with Greg Ripley-Duggan, on 17 May 2005 (previews from 14 May), with the following cast:

LAPO	Ron Cook
LOTI	Ralf Little
POPE JULIUS II	David Frederickson
CARDINAL	Luke Healy

Director   Jennie Darnell
Designer   Matthew Wright
Lighting Designer   Neil Austin
Composer   Adam Cork
Sound Designer   Fergus O'Hare

The production transferred to the Garrick Theatre, London, presented by Greg Ripley-Duggan with Robert Cogo-Fawcett, on 12 September 2005 (previews from 30 August).

On the Ceiling is from an idea by Joshua Richards and Alan Osborne.

Nigel Planer would like to thank Ron Cook, Ralf Little and Jennie Darnell.

Characters

LOTI (Lodovico del Buono)

LAPO (Lapo d'Antonio)

POPE

CARDINAL

ACT ONE

*A bright autumn morning, 1508. First light. We are on a
wooden scaffolding platform, high up, where the vaulted walls
become the ceiling of the Sistine Chapel.*

*The set is a raised wooden platform which is supported on
large wooden beams. Upstage-right there is an opening in the
platform floor from which a ladder goes downwards
underneath the platform. The back wall curves steeply up and
then out towards the audience at about fifteen feet above the
platform. There might be a further ladder and wooden
scaffolding propped against this back wall. The back wall has
been freshly plastered and has a beautiful pinky-white hue to
it. At the left and right edges of the wall might be the
suggestion of other colours, shapes even. The front edges of the
platform which forms the stage, and the curved back wall – the
bits facing the audience – should not be neatly finished, but
give the impression that we are looking at a cross-section. In
other words, the platform would in reality continue right out
across the auditorium.*

*A basket appears from the upstage-right opening, flung up
there by someone below who is climbing up the ladder from
underneath the platform. A man climbs up out of the opening
and onto the stage – LOTI. He is seriously out of breath, so
pauses at the top of the ladder and heaves for air. He
continues up and out onto the stage, where he leans over and
wheezes. After a pause he is followed by a second man –
LAPO, who is carrying more things. Many more things. A
satchel with a water bottle, two bags, a basket – he looks like a
beast of burden. He too is seriously out of breath, but he is not
wheezing like LOTI. They stand or sit for a few moments trying
to catch their breath.*

*Although dressed in what – if one could see them – are the
clothes of sixteenth-century Italians, they could be from any
age, or even any planet because they are both covered virtually*

from head to foot in dried spatters of plaster and paint. Their hair should have plaster dust in it, their clothes are almost solid with it, like a white armour casing or strange spacesuits. In short they look like typical cowboy plasterers and painter-decorators from any age.

LAPO, *the older of the two, is the first to recover enough to speak.*

LAPO (*breathless* . . . and another thing . . . I think you'll find is . . . if there's one thing . . . worth learning . . . in the world . . . it's that there's definitely . . .

LOTI *is lying on the floor, wheezing loudly.*

. . . you made me forget now . . .

LOTI. I . . . chest . . . mmm . . . oof! . . .

LAPO *has to unpack all their stuff on his own because LOTI is still breathless, almost asthmatic.*

LAPO. Oi! Were you actually going to help me with this, or . . . ?

LOTI. I am . . . I am . . .

LAPO. You are? You are . . . what? An indolent sponge?

LOTI (*still out of breath*). I am helping . . . just . . .

LAPO. Respect. That's what's worth learning. Respect.

LOTI *gets up and, in trying to help, accidentally knocks a canvas sack of something down the trap hole. He recoils from the opening, scared of the height. This reaction knocks another two bags of powder down the trap. If possible, there is a chain reaction, and the entire contents of a box slides off a shelf and down the trap.*

LOTI. Oh.

LAPO. Now look what you done!

LOTI. Do I have to? Look, I mean. I don't like the height.

LAPO. Great big wuss!

LAPO is finishing unpacking their gear and starts to look around him, realising that they are alone on the platform. This does not please him. LOTI dares, gingerly, to look back down the trap.

LOTI. Actually, it looks quite good.

LAPO. Huh.

LOTI. Hey, maybe we should paint the floor instead.

LAPO is very agitated that they are alone.

LAPO. Oh no. Not again. Where is she? Where is she, the spaggot?

LOTI. Oh, what's the matter with the master now?

LAPO. She's a Florentine spaggot, that's what's the matter.

LOTI. Could've got stuck behind an ox-cart.

LAPO. What?

LOTI. There's a lot of oxen out there today. Lot of congestion.

LAPO. Nah. She's having another terribilatah, isn't she? She's on a wobblioni, that's what she's on. Third time in a month. How long is this going to go on?

LOTI (*looking up at the vaulted back wall*). Aww. Look at that. Perfect that. Smooth and flat and a little bit brilliant. Beautiful.

LAPO. I just can't believe it. Who does Michelangelo think she fucking is? (*Throws down his own bag in disgust.*)

LOTI (*still out of breath*). Lovely. Aren't you? Look at that. You know what? (*To LAPO.*) We are the last gorgeousness on God's stinking earth. (*Blows a kiss at the wall.*) Mwah! Beautiful!

LAPO. How wet? (*He goes over and touches it.*) Bastard!!! She's got three hours, four hours maximum. Why is she doing this to us??

LOTI. Maybe she doesn't quite feel it today.

LAPO. Feel it? *Feel* it?? She's a mincing, sidewinding, farting little crab and I'm going to shove this . . . (*He picks up a stick with a wedge of felt on the end of it*.) . . . right up her snotty little twadge when she gets here.

LOTI. Well, what do we do then? Take the rest of the day off? Shall we?

LAPO. Good idea. You wait there. I'll see if I can get someone to carry all your stuff back down for you.

LOTI. Really?

LAPO. No. Not really. Spaggot! We work.

LOTI (*disappointed*). Oh. But what about the master?

LAPO. Well, since she hasn't told us what she wants, we'll just have to get *everything* ready. The lot.

LOTI. What? Can't we just put our feet up for a bit? I'm knackered.

LAPO. Already? You've hardly put on your shirt and shoes today!

LOTI. Yeah, well, you didn't drink what I did last night.

LAPO. I have *never* drunk what you did last night. Even in the bloom of youth. Come on! Slugabed! Move your pasty carcass!

LOTI. Surely you were never young, old man?

LAPO. I was! Just wasn't a waster. By the time I was your age I'd mixed pigments on three Annunciations!

During the following dialogue, LAPO goes to the various baskets and canvas bags and gets out packets of powders. LOTI pours water into a jug. Occasionally LAPO will toss something to LOTI, who catches it almost automatically, without looking – a brush, a rag, and eventually some eggs. LOTI mixes eggs and prepares to grind charcoal. All this is done without their conscious attention while they talk – as if they were driving a car – it is their regular start-up routine for work. The more unspoken co-operation between them the better, with a suggestion at all times that LAPO is the superior, with LOTI – for all his skills – the assistant.

And now look at me! Working for a man with less experience than a fruit fly. How am I supposed to respect that? I wouldn't mind if the dozy arse-wipe knew *anything* about what she was doing. Wouldn't be so bad. I could bear that. I could respect that. But this . . . (*Looks around at the ceiling.*) . . . this is a fucking fiasco.

LOTI. A fresco fiasco. Hey, that rhymes!

LAPO. No it doesn't! . . . It alliterates.

LOTI. We done a good job, though – with that wall. That is lovely, that wall. Lovely and flat. Have you had a proper feel of that? Uh? Go on. Touch it again.

LAPO. What's the point? What is the fucking point?

LAPO *throws eggs across to* LOTI *who expertly cracks one or two of them into a jar.*

She knows nothing about slaking, floating, skimming, pouncing, scoring. Nothing. And nothing about eggs.

LOTI (*expertly cracking another one into the jar*). Well, I don't know much about eggs.

LAPO. That's cos you're an ignorant piss-ant – and anyway, you do know about eggs. Would you use a country egg or a Roman egg, or any town egg – even a Florentine egg – to touch up that young cherub's beautiful arse over there? (*He points out into the auditorium.*)

LOTI. Town egg, of course. Lovely 'n' milky a town egg'd be.

LAPO. There, you know about eggs. All you need to know about eggs. More than Michelangelo. (*He puts on a camp impersonation.*) 'I'm not really a painter, you know.' Telling me. (*He minces about and* LOTI *laughs.*) 'I'm a sculptor, not a painter. Painting is so . . . somehow . . . lesser. Less than lasting. I didn't really want this job, you know, I'm a sculptor.'

LOTI. Who's that supposed to be? That's rubbish, that is.

LAPO (*still impersonating*). 'I wanted to carve the Pope's tomb! I already bought the marble!'

LOTI (*laughing*). That's nothing like him.

LAPO (*still impersonating*). 'Do you know who I am? Do you know who I am?'

LOTI. You're a sculptor.

LAPO (*as himself again*). Pompous knobhead. If you want to create anything, make anything, you have to *forget* who you are. That's the whole point.

LOTI. That's so true. Who said that?

LAPO. I forget.

They continue working for a moment. Then . . .

LOTI (*feeding him*). So, what's it like being the master then? Torture is it?

LAPO (*back in his impersonation*). 'Ah! Why am I tortured in this way? Tell me. I work harder than anyone who has ever lived, and now this . . . this . . . ceiling. Why me? Hounded, that's what I am, hounded.'

LOTI joins in with 'hounded' and laughs like a child.

'Right, that's it! I'm being laughed at! You're fired! You're both fired! You're *all* fired!!! Just bugger off and leave me alone!'

LOTI (*laughing at the impersonation*). That is *so* bad.

LOTI laughs but does not move to go and carries on grinding charcoal. LAPO, in his impersonation, is now in a spitting queeny rage.

LAPO. 'Right! Right! That's *it*! I'm leaving! You can sort out Noah and the Flood amongst yourselves! I'm finishing now! I'm actually going! Now!'

LAPO actually gets a few stairs down the ladder at the trap. LOTI puts one of the cloth bags on his head so it looks a bit like a pope's mitre. He speaks in a silly booming pope-type voice, but his rendition is wooden and flat. He doesn't mind at all being the less able performer of the two.

LOTI. 'Not so fast, chum. Just one minute, matey. You can't just leave like that. In fact, I order you to stay.'

LAPO. 'I'm a sculptor, I'm a sculptor, I'm a sculptor!'

LOTI. 'Well, I'm the fucking Pope! Tch! You artists, with your temperamental mood swings.'

LAPO. Exactly. I'll teach him how to feel it.

LAPO has dropped his impersonation. He chucks an item which was in his hand to LOTI, who catches it without looking. LOTI takes off his pope hat. LAPO spits on the floor with venom. The preparations for work are complete. LAPO takes a breath, a long slow breath and wipes his hands on a cleanish rag. LOTI watches him like a sheep dog, keenly awaiting further instructions. LAPO contemplates the ceiling, the opposite wall (auditorium) and the back wall in silence. There is a pause while LAPO looks out across the auditorium.

(Pointing to back of the auditorium and whistling through his teeth and shaking his head like a typical builder.) See that? That is shoddy crappy work, that.

They both look out across the auditorium.

LOTI. We did that bit . . . actually.

LAPO. Fuck off! No, what I mean is why are we here? Eh? Why? To save his poncy backside, that's why.

LAPO runs his palm over the back wall and pauses for thought. He puts his cheek to the wall. Gently, he feels around the plaster. This ritual should have the gravity of a wine-tasting, or a safe-cracking. All the while LOTI is focused on LAPO, waiting for his expert opinion. LAPO looks again at the size of the area of blank plaster on the wall behind them and the vaulted ceiling above and for a moment makes silent calculations.

This beauty won't be worth painting on in four hours. We'll have to hack it all off.

LOTI *(knackered at the prospect)*. Doh. Not again. We'll get all dusty.

LAPO. Don't you start bellyaching!

LOTI. No, it's my chest . . .

LAPO. What do you think he wanted up here? If he'd deigned to turn up, that is.

LOTI. We can't just put stuff up there without the master.

LAPO. Yeah, well, he hasn't showed up, has he? Having another hufferini. Let's see what he's drawn here at least. Come on.

LOTI. Do we have to?

LAPO. No, we don't have to. We are merely curious as to the crackpot intentions of the nincompoop to whom we are contracted.

LOTI. Are we?

LAPO. Yes, we are. Come on.

LOTI. Alright. I don't mind looking at drawings.

LAPO goes to a pile of what look like rolls of wallpaper and large architect's plans, and starts to sift through them, making a mess, unrolling some, unfolding others, to see what drawings they contain. LOTI *follows him.*

LAPO (*considering a drawing*). . . . No . . . (*And another.*) . . . no . . . no.

LAPO passes LOTI *the end of one and they unroll it a few feet to look. We don't see what is on it. They look up to the vault as if to calculate if the drawing will fit in the space above them. During this sequence* LAPO *occasionally slaps or pushes* LOTI *in order to remain in charge.* LAPO *sees the drawings with increasing distaste – they didn't draw like this in the good old days. He tuts.*

BOTH. Nope.

They roll it up and get another one out. It doesn't fit either, they try holding it sideways, upside down, etc.

Nope.

LAPO (*tutting*). Tch tch. See that? (*Indicating one of the drawings.*) You should never twist a torso like that.

They chuck it down and get another from the pile. They start to unroll it but get no further than a couple of feet before it is obviously wrong.

BOTH. Naaaah.

LAPO (*sighing*). Oh dear.

They chuck this roll down as well. This time they both go to different rolls. Something on one of the rolls attracts LOTI's attention.

LOTI. Phwooooaarrr! Look at this! (*He unrolls a bit more. It contains something rude.*) Woaaahh! Well, it's very . . . erm . . . (*Tilts his head to see if he has the image upside down.*)

LAPO joins him. They unroll it completely. It looks as if it could be the face of Eve, nestling in Adam's naked thighs.

LAPO. May God forgive us!

LOTI. Has she just. . . . ? . . . *and* with him? . . . at the same time?

LAPO (*finally*). Well, you wouldn't get that in a Raphael.

LAPO walks to the front of the stage and sits, looking out in disgust. LOTI reluctantly rolls up the drawing, but continues to unroll others to see if they might fit.

I admit to being somewhat confused, Loti, by the predicament in which, unwillingly, we find ourselves. See that down there? (*He looks down through a gap in the floorboards downstage-left.*) That is Jesus handing over the keys to St Peter, that is.

LOTI (*reluctant to go too near the gap in the floor*). Oh yeah, brilliant that one. Perugino, Boticelli, Ghirlandaio, the lot. Took seven weeks that, I heard.

LAPO. St Peter is buried underneath us right now. Right down there. We're virtually sitting on top of him.

LOTI (*finding a drawing he thinks may fit*). This might be the one. What do you think? Lapo?

LAPO. As far as holy places go, this is sort of it. The one. They don't get more in the way of holiness than this. And yet we are putting things on the ceiling that I wouldn't want my mother to see.

LOTI. Well, she's not going to see it, is she? Well, not close up anyway. And it's not as bad as that one we did last Tuesday – that cherub sticking his fingers up the Cumean sybil. That was fucking outrageous.

LAPO. God will see it!

LOTI. Yeah, that's true, I suppose. And the Pope probably. And that could be bad. For us, I mean. You don't want to mess with old Julius.

LAPO. Always us – the splodge, the chips, the grinders, the muratore, the pontarolos. Always down to us in the end. Who makes all this? And this? (*Indicates all around him.*) Who actually makes it, eh? I have sons, you know. Sons for my sins.

LOTI. Yeah, but it's not our fault, is it, if the master wants to burn in Hell for eternity, that's up to him, isn't it? We just put it up there.

LAPO. 'And I will descend upon you in your scurrility and your filth and upon your palaces and your whores unless you repent!' You ever actually hear Savonorola preach? I did. '93.

LOTI. '93? Hmm. I'd've been about seven, old man.

LAPO. 'And a fire will come to tear all your fine clothes and pompousness and lascivious books and images of nudity. (LAPO *is impersonating the preacher Savonorola, who was burnt at the stake in Florence twelve years previously.*) And gather them together into a pyre and burn these Vanities in one big Fire!'

LOTI. I mean, *we're* not going to be burnt to a twig in Hell, are we? No one will even know it was us, will they? We didn't even draw the bleeding stuff. It's not our ideas. We just do what the master wants, we . . . facilitate. God will understand the difference. Surely.

LAPO. 'And what'ere images ye make shall be damned for all eternity –'

LOTI. I suppose it all depends on what you mean by 'make'. We didn't *design* it, did we? Except for Noah's hand.

LAPO. What about Noah's hand?

LOTI. Well, I thought you did a bloody good job of that, even though I say so myself.

LAPO. Well yes, of course . . . We are all guilty. We are all responsible. And besides, somebody had to show her how to do it. Minging little tart.

LOTI. That was brilliant, that hand. (*He looks across stage left and up and out to see the hand on the Noah segment which was painted some weeks/months ago.*)

LAPO (*looks to the sky*). God look down on us and forgive us our small part – our facilitation, our servile contribution to the insane and tortured fantasising of this . . . this . . . this Florentine. He made us do it. We had no choice. We only obey orders. Even when they are given us by a complete wanker who couldn't even mix up an ultramarine.

LOTI. Yeah, but he's pretty good at foreshortening, isn't he?

LAPO. Not as good as Leonardo.

LOTI. Don't let him hear you say that.

LAPO. Now there's a man. A man among men, da Vinci. There . . . is an artist. A true painter. In terms of composition, meaning, lifelike representations, backgrounds, colour. *And* he can bend a horseshoe with his bare hands.

LOTI. Ah, but come on, Milly can draw. You have to give him that.

LAPO. You ever seen a Durer?

LOTI. Well, I meant . . . for an Italian, right? Milly can draw for an Italian, you can't deny that.

LAPO. Who had to tell him how to plan a giornata, so you don't put up more skim coat than you can paint in a day?

LOTI. We did. You did.

LAPO. Who mixes his colours, prepares his brushes, transfers
the cartoons, times his intonacoes . . .

LOTI. You do. We do.

LAPO (*impersonating Michelangelo again*). 'What do I do
with this, Lapo? How do I get this . . . (*Picks up a roll and
minces across stage.*) . . . up there? I'm not the right man
for the job.'

LAPO *is about to hand the rolled-up cartoon back to* LOTI
when he has an idea.

Come on.

LOTI. What are you doing?

LAPO. Let's just stick this rude one right up here.

LAPO *starts to unroll the rude cartoon against the back
wall.* LOTI *stops him. There is a silly scuffle.*

LOTI. Stop! Stop! Stop!

LAPO. Why? Why not? He don't care!

LOTI. Because it doesn't fit here. Look, it's meant for up there.
See.

He unrolls the rude cartoon to show LAPO *where it might
go. It is a section of Adam and Eve in the garden of Eden,
showing Eve's face turning away from Adam's thighs and
penis.*

I reckon that . . . is . . . Eve . . . taking a breather . . . hurr,
hurr.

LAPO (*referring to the tiny penis in the picture*). Or eating a
walnut.

LOTI *searches among the other rolls and finding the one he
picked out before, takes it to the back wall.*

LOTI. I reckon it's this one . . . that's meant to go up here.
Look, that . . . matches . . . with . . . that. (*Looking at the
drawing and the wall offstage left.*) . . . another prophet . . .
see?

LOTI *seems to have a better grasp of the intended structure of the piece.* LAPO *is grudgingly impressed.*

LAPO. Oh. Mmm. Alright. Well done.

LAPO *returns some of the rolls of paper to the basket.*

Perhaps Julius should've asked you in at the planning stage.

LOTI. How d'you mean?

LAPO. Well, he's not going to like all this, is he? The old Pope. All these prophets and sybils and that. He'll want lots of expensive clothes and jewels up there, and pictures of himself. And gold. Like it should be.

LOTI. Well, I think Milly's trying to do something a bit different.

LAPO. Well, I think he hasn't got a clue. Come on. Let's get on and do the holes. At least something will be done professionally.

LOTI. Really? Without the master?

LAPO. If something isn't up here soon we'll have to hack it all off and start again anyway.

LOTI. Alright. (*He starts to clear the table. He is smiling inanely.*)

LAPO. What are you grinning for?

LOTI. I like doing the holes.

LAPO. Oh good. That's the most important thing. That you should be happy in your work. Now, are you sitting comfortably?

LOTI. Yes thanks.

LAPO. Good. Then we can begin. Spaggot! (*Smacks* LOTI *across the head.*)

During the following dialogue they unroll the cartoon, which has lines and greyed-in areas all over it, and flatten it over a trestle table. Using a stylus or bradl, they punch holes along the lines. Following his line, LOTI's hand bumps into LAPO's.

Get over your own side! (*Then, while working.*) Once again, Michelangelo's arse is saved . . . Once more, and against our better judgement, we allow our superior skill and knowledge to be used – abused, I mean – at the hands of a dilettante, a trifler, a pottering Sunday painter, an *amateur*. That's what he is, an *am-a-teur*.

LOTI. I wish we were working for Raphael. I tried to get us in there but no joy. You're too good, that was the trouble. Too much of a threat.

LAPO. Always the way. (*Still thinking about Michelangelo.*) Our master's an amateur. He doesn't pay us – he stashes his money away in the Maria Nuova –

LOTI. Really? I didn't know that.

LAPO. Oh yes! 1,500 ducats he's had so far! Already! And where is it? Eh? That's what we'd all like to know. And he's put at least half of that away.

LOTI. How do you know?

LAPO. Well, how much has he paid you so far?

LOTI. Only materials and lodgings.

LAPO. Exactly my point. And he's bought a farm and woolshop for his brother outside Florence. (*Impersonating again.*) 'I'm only doing this to support my brothers and my poor old father in Settignano.' Bollocks. Oh, you don't think he's doing this for love, do you?

LOTI. No, he's doing this because the Pope ordered him to, poor bastard. He tried to get out of it three times. He wanted to do the tomb instead. You told me that.

LAPO. Oh come on, Loti! He's loaded! He's in it for the dosh, mate! Same as you and me, except we *have* to work to live; he's got enough hidden away to last the rest of his life. He could retire to the Tuscan hills right now if he wanted, sitting in an olive grove – live out his days under the Sangiovese vine, in a wicker chair, watching sunsets, nice glass of Chianti in his hand. Young girls tending to his every whim . . . except he probably wouldn't want that last bit.

They work in silence for a few moments.

LOTI. You know they have wine in the lunch breaks in the Raphael rooms.

LAPO. Ha! Doesn't surprise me.

LOTI. Come to that, they *have* lunch breaks. Wish we had lunch breaks. And they were all paid a sub. Weeks ago.

LAPO. I wouldn't mind if the little angel could fresco, but he's an amateur.

LOTI. Well, he doesn't have the experience. He needs you to show him how.

LAPO. Yes, but that's my point. What happened with the Noah and the Flood should never have been allowed to happen. Never.

LOTI. He was finding his feet, I suppose.

LAPO (*with vehemence*). He painted onto soaking wet skim, Loti! There was mildew. Mildew! I told him, but he went ahead and did it. Just trying to save on limecast, the niggardly pinchfist. How long did it take to put right?

LOTI. Three weeks.

LAPO. Three arsing weeks! It's us who take the stick for that. It's our reputations on the line too, you know.

LOTI. Yeah. Wanker. Mind you, I wouldn't be able to do what he does with a great chunk of marble. Nor would you . . . Would you, Lapo? Be able to carve sublime images out of stone? . . . Lapo? . . . Would you? . . .

LAPO. The man's a passenger. A fucking disgrace. Pouncer. (*'Pouncer' is an order to* LOTI.)

LOTI. Can't I finish the hand?

LAPO. No. Make me a pouncing bag. Please.

After cheekily finishing the hand in a hurry, LOTI *goes to prepare a pouncing bag, which is a small tied piece of muslin cloth containing ground-up charcoal.*

(*While focusing on the work.*) What gets me is our lack of choice. Not only the choice of whether to work or not, but the choice of what to put in that work.

LAPO *changes ends on the cartoon, and continues to punch holes.*

If you actually don't have to work, if you have enough in the Maria Nuova bank, you can decide where it is worth putting your talent – putting your time even. Your opinion matters. Your judgement is a currency. The rest of us do not weigh in on the scales of history. We are a service industry to those living on interest, or rent, or on payments for work already done . . . property already owned. Our very seed dispensible. We are dried up on the crisp handkerchief of history – a shoddy, peevish, furtive little toss-off.

LOTI. Yeah. Did you know Raphael is using *naked* women as models?

LAPO. Uh?

LOTI. No. Straight up. He's using live women, like real ones. But with no clothes on!! And then – like – drawing them. Among other things.

They continue to work, but LOTI *cannot stop thinking about the women.*

Yeah, evidently he had five of them in his studio the other day, and he drew the eyes of one, the nose of another, the chin of another and so on . . . you know . . . downwards. All so that he could draw one perfect woman. I wish we could do that.

LAPO. No chance, son.

LOTI. Yeah, it's a bit of a pisser really, isn't it? Raphael takes five amazing looking birds to make one perfect beauty and we get Tommasso de Cavalieri modelling not just the men on the ceiling, but all the women too. With oranges stuck on his chest.

LAPO. I told you, we are flunkies to a Florentine poof. A sodomising, dried-fruit-exploring, back-entrance user.

LOTI. What? You can't say things like that!

LAPO. What?

LOTI. You look really ugly when you do that.

LAPO. What d'you mean?

LOTI. Well, even if he wasn't, you know – and you don't know for sure that he is actually – it wouldn't necessarily make him any better at fresco.

LAPO. Are you saying that I am unfairly judging our employer on account of his concupiscent proclivities?

LOTI. Erm, yeah. That, and you being jealous of him for having more vision than you. Really ugly, that.

LAPO. Thank you for that coruscating insight, Loti. May I have the charcoal pouncing bag now, if you'd be so kind?

LOTI. What?

LAPO (*barking*). Charcoal!!

LOTI passes LAPO the pouncing bag for him to test.

LOTI. Anyway, I think his mind is on higher things.

LAPO. His mind may well be.

LAPO pats it against his hand to satisfy himself it is working. He blows on his hand to test the grind of the charcoal.

LOTI. And in the Raphael rooms they don't have to climb up 323 steps to get to work. They can just turn up, completely hungover if they feel like it – still pissed even – walk straight up to the wall, and just . . . start. (*Pause.*) They must look up at us on their way in and think –

LAPO (*between breaths, blowing the charcoal*). Fucking – 'ugly' – amateur – wedge-wangling scumbuckets – that's what they think.

LOTI. I was going to say 'poor bastards', that's what they must think. (*Pause.*) And they got paid three months upfront.

LAPO. How do you know?

LOTI. The other day I was in The Cardinal's Arms and I was talking to my mate Briacci – oh! and there was this woman in there, she was an absolutely, slide-off-the-frying-pan hot brass! I mean she had it – (*He mimes low neckline.*) up front, round the back, and the skin! (*He shudders.*) The clothes on her must've cost a few hundred! And the smell of her! Wow! Anyway . . .

LAPO. *You* got near enough to get a sniff? Spolvero. (*'Spolvero' is an order to* LOTI.)

During the following dialogue they perform the spolvero. Firstly, they take the cartoon and flatten it against the wall. LAPO gets some nails and will bang them gently into the 'rough coat' area around the outside edges of the cartoon.

LOTI. Yeah. Well, no at first, but, I was talking to Briacci – he's my mate from Raphael's lot downstairs, you know. That's how come I know what's going on down there. And they get free cakes at six o'clock down there!! Can you believe it!!

They are ready to nail the cartoon. They both produce hammers from their apron pockets. LAPO's is a proper one, suitable for the job. LOTI's is small and delicate, probably from his silversmithing days. When the cartoon is up flat against the back wall, LAPO begins to pat and blow charcoal gently into all of the little holes he has punched into the cartoon on the back wall.

LAPO. And this bit of stuff? What about her?

LOTI. Well, I'm talking away to Briacci, right, who I haven't seen in ages, not since Bologna. You know they melted down his bronze Apollo to make a canon to blast the French. Poor guy. He spent seven months on that.

A pause while they work.

LAPO. So you didn't get near the skirt. You saw her and she looked better than your mother – you thought in your drunken state – it is quite dark in there. You imagined you smelt her – and that's your story?

LOTI. No, no. Wait. So we haven't seen each other for a while, right, so Briacci tells me he's doing the Raphael rooms and I tell him I'm on the ceiling – and the moment *she* hears that, I saw her ears prick up, and her back stiffen and she shot me a glance – sort of sized me up.

LAPO. . . . quickly realised that you have an overripe and putrid courgette between your legs, laughed a little to herself and you went home for a bit of left-handed contemplation.

LOTI. No – she's looking at me in a funny sort of way. Sort of hot and prickly and I can see her neck start pumping gently. She actually catches my eye and the corner of her mouth curls up in a secret little smile that no one else will see.

LAPO. What was the matter with her? Short-sighted or just mentally subnormal?

LOTI. Hurr hurr. (*Laughing sheepishly.*) That's what I thought. But then she comes over! And it turns out she thinks I'm him! The master!

LAPO. What? How come? Even you don't look as bad as that. Actually, on second thoughts . . .

LOTI. Well, I know I'm no oil painting. (*Guiltily.*) Could have been the red and gold jacket I was wearing . . .

LAPO (*shocked*). What? So you've been dressing up as a Florentine and hanging around in bars pretending to be Michelangelo so that you can ensnare unsuspecting trouts?

LOTI. No. I didn't tell her I was him!

LAPO. Right. Good.

LOTI. Well. (*Embarrassed.*) I didn't tell her I wasn't him, either.

LAPO. What do you mean by that?

LOTI. She was all over me, Lapo. It was great. It was . . . intense.

LAPO. I bet it fucking was. So did you drag her back to the kennel and stomp her, then? Oh no, I forgot you share your bed with three ten-year-old fruit sellers and a chicken. And where was I? How come I didn't hear you come in?

LOTI. It wasn't like that.

LAPO. You mean she took you back to her luxury apartment on the Via Tornabuoni and – after wisely hosing you down with vinegar – tried to massage your little anchovy into a hake.

LOTI. No, it wasn't like that, Lapo. I meant the *conversation* was intense. She touched my elbow for a second or two and she looked into my eyes with a look that . . . oh, I can't describe it to you. I've never known anything like it, Laps – they were like lakes in the moonlight, her eyes.

LAPO. You mean she looked into Milly's eyes. She looked into the eyes of a man with a staff of twenty who he still hasn't paid. She looked into the eyes of a man with a farm and a woolshop in Settignano, and a couple of thousand ducats in the Maria Nuova, and it made her hot.

LOTI. No, she was looking into the eyes of a great artist.

LAPO. Aaargghh! A great artist? Give us a break! Ghirlandaio, Ghiberti, Gozzoli . . . Raphael, *maybe*. But Milly? Famous, I'll grant you. But great?

LOTI. I mean someone she *thought* was a great artist and for a moment, I was . . . (*He is lost for words.*) Intense, that's what it was. It was as if I could feel the pulsating beat of life itself.

LAPO. Lodovico, with an apprentice, one looks for qualities such as diligence, application, talent, and generally tries to avoid the kind of person who dresses up in bars.

LOTI. I wasn't exactly dressing up. Could've just been my natural animal charisma that did it.

A pause while they work.

LAPO. You know, when we get thrown out of Rome for your feeble attempts at impersonation, and we have to tour around with the Canzone Theatre telling our story to all the other out-of-work artists for the price of a meal, I'll thank you that after my fourteen-year apprenticeship in fresco, I ended up with a dickhead plasterer doing a cheap comic turn in some northern alehouse.

LOTI (*laughing stupidly*). Yeah, we could do the Pope and the Sculptor as a double act.

LAPO. Please. I was being sarcastic.

LOTI. 'Bless you, bless you and all my artisans, bless them all. Even if they do have to earn a crust passing on the latest news instead of actually doing it. Bless them.'

LAPO. I would rather go and make bricks from my own shit than be a turn in the Canzone.

LOTI. Oh, I don't know. I heard that Leonardo's lot earned more money during the Canzone tour, talking about how they made it, than they ever did actually painting 'The Last Supper'! Quite fancy myself as a comedian.

LAPO. Well, you may need to be. (*Then referring to the work they are doing.*) Now, are you ready?

They have finished the spolvero. LOTI joins LAPO to take out the nails and pull the cartoon down.

LOTI (*pointing to part of the cartoon*). Missed a bit.

LAPO. I know that.

LAPO finishes the charcoaling and, together, they peel the paper cartoon off the wall. LAPO dusts the excess charcoal from the cartoon with a feather handed to him by LOTI. They stand back to look at the wall which is now a mass of little dots rather like an astrological diagram. LAPO nips back to the wall to wipe a bit then steps back out again.

That's the business.

LOTI. Magic, eh?

LAPO. No. Not magic. Just dogged adherence to time-honoured technique.

LOTI starts to clear away the used cartoon. LAPO stands with his charcoal-covered hands in the air like a surgeon about to go to theatre.

So, this pulsating beat of life. Was your lover girl aware of it too? Or was it just pulsating quietly to itself under your tunic?

LOTI. No, I told you, I wasn't even . . . you know. In a way, though, that was what made the moment so special – our connection was more sort of spiritual, like Plato says.

LAPO. Ah, Plato was there too, was he? But you still went home to bang the bishop.

LOTI. No, I didn't! Well, not until aft– Anyway, it's not the point of the story, what happened afterwards . . . Or didn't happen afterwards, I mean. At all.

LAPO. No, the point of your story is that it doesn't matter how many years you train, how righteous your conduct – if you're rich and famous you can pull the seafood.

LOTI. No, I told you. We just talked. About frescoes, actually. She knew a lot, Lapo. I think she knows Raphael too.

LAPO (*suddenly serious*). How does she know Raphael? I mean, how well? You didn't tell her what's on the ceiling did you?

LOTI. Naaooo.

LAPO. So, she was one of Raphael's tarts?

LOTI. Well, I don't know that for sure.

LAPO. No, you don't! You don't know anything! You could've really dropped us in the shit! You're my responsibility, you know! She was most likely a spy for Raphael or Bramante – they'd *kill* to know what we're putting up here. Just as well you didn't get out your sad root vegetable. It's not just semen that gets spilt on the sheets, you know. Idiot.

LOTI. Erm . . . (*Guiltily.*) I hope she wasn't a spy actually.

LAPO. Oh, I get it. Oh, that's magnificent, that is. That's us finished then, isn't it? Pfft! So you told her all the secrets?

LOTI. Well . . . not all.

LAPO. . . . What's on the ceiling.

LOTI. Well . . . only what we done so far.

LAPO. . . . And she tells Raphael.

LOTI. You think she would?

LAPO. . . . She tells Bramante and we're history, mate. You really are a pillock, you know that? I sometimes wonder what idiocy possessed me to take you on. And you didn't even get your leg over!

LOTI. D'you really think that's what she was after?

LAPO. We're looking at a life on the road, mate. Better start practising your acting skills.

LOTI. But they wouldn't just use people like that, would they? I mean, nick ideas so blatantly like that?

LAPO. Ha. Depends what it's worth. I'll say one thing for Milly, at least he's original – mad as a tadpole's fart – but original.

LOTI. . . . Erm. Do you think I should go back there, find her, and tell her that I was, like, making it all up?

LAPO. No. I think you should place your knob in the hinge of that ladder there and close it, slowly. It would cause less pain, in the long run.

LOTI. Yes. Well, I'm really sorry. I just got a bit carried away. I mean, she was so beautiful, you know. It's hard to believe that something that looks as good as that could be so nasty.

Beat. LAPO *starts to clear the platform and put some of the pigments in order.*

LAPO. You can take breakfast now if you want.

LOTI. You really going to finish it then? . . .

LAPO. Since the master is still on his wobblioni.

LOTI. D'you want any breakfast?

LAPO. No, I'm not eating.

LAPO *smoothes his hand over the wet plaster.* LOTI *goes to one of the baskets they brought with them.*

LOTI. But what about colours? I can't sit by and eat while you mix your own pigments up.

LAPO. Oh fuck off. Better than you anyway.

LOTI. Not.

LAPO. Am.

LOTI. Not.

LAPO. Am.

LOTI. Not.

LAPO. Am. Oh, just eat your frigging onion and let me get on with the man's work.

LOTI. Not.

> LOTI *takes an onion and a bit of bread out of the basket and starts to eat.* LAPO *continues to clean the platform, clearing off rags and scraps of paper. He tosses a couple of bits of the scrumpled paper over the edge of the upstage-right hole in the platform and stops to watch as (unseen by us) they drift down to the floor, hundreds of feet below.*

> I wish you wouldn't do that. Makes my balls go funny. Being reminded of the height.

LAPO. Well, you're in the wrong job then, mate, aren't you?

LOTI (*cheerfully*). Oh, I know that. But I didn't have much choice because I was thrown out of Bertoldo the silversmith's.

LAPO. What was that for again? Impersonating a master jeweller to ingratiate yourself with the foundry boys?

> LAPO *continues to toss pieces of paper over the edge and watch them fall. He then takes a broom and starts to sweep the area in front of the wall clean.*

LOTI. Not exactly. You know I can't work with smelting wax. Disagrees with my chest.

LAPO. I saved your rump, son. I picked you out of the sulphury slime, and rescued you from a life of asphyxiating monotony. Perhaps I should send you back there too.

LOTI. Oh no. Don't do that. I won't talk to a pretty woman ever again – ever . . . I wonder if all of Raphael's women are spies.

LAPO. One perfect woman, eh? So Raphael thinks that he can make one perfect beauty. You know what Plato actually said? He said we all desire to be immortal through beauty. Some of us fall for the beauty of reproduction – having kids. That's what you get if you go after women. That's the mistake I made. Who knows what I might be now if I'd managed to resist that one . . . But then, there's another kind who seek immortality through ideas, or poems . . . or painting. Or sculpture even. Like Milly. No babies, no children. No offspring for them, no continual gnawing anxiety. Oh no, they don't have sons to care for, mouths to feed. No, they make *discourse*, they make Art. They get to have *vision*. They transfer all their desire onto a church wall or a ceiling. They bring something of wonder to birth in the presence of beauty.

LOTI. How d'you know all that?

LAPO. I've done the trivium, mate. Grammar, logic, rhetoric.

LOTI. Bloody hell! Woo-hoo! You never told me that! Who was your teacher? Anyone famous?

LAPO. No, I taught myself.

LOTI. Really? Where?

LAPO *goes back to the canvas bags and pots. He looks for something and chucks aside more of the scrumpled paper.*

LAPO. In the upstairs room of a butcher's shop in Urbino if you really want to know. Before I was thirty. I didn't have the San Marco gardens of the Medici to wander around like our beloved guardian Angelo, but I did my best to 'humanise' myself, as they say. Anyway, you can't teach someone to be wise. Wisdom cannot be taught, only rediscovered within. You can't teach someone virtue. Plato said that too, as a matter of fact.

LOTI. Hey, you're good. You're very good.

LAPO. Not that it did me any good, though.

LOTI. How d'you mean?

LAPO. Too much reason. It's like another bloody voice in you head. Arguing with God. All the time. Na na na naa. Na na na naa. Never stops.

LOTI. Oh. I didn't know it did *that*.

LAPO. Still, at least now when I'm being burnt on a stake in Hell, I'll understand *why*.

LAPO *is angry at not finding what he is looking for among the pots.*

LOTI (*with his mouth full*). What's up?

LAPO. Where's the blue?

LOTI. No blue?

LAPO. No blue.

LOTI. No blue. Forgot to tell you. Too expensive. Milly said it has to come from the Jesuits of the San Giusto alle Mura. He was telling me he didn't want to spend any more at this stage.

LAPO. What?

LOTI. He didn't want to spend any . . . more . . . money . . . at this . . . stage.

LAPO. What is going on here? What the fuck is going on? We save his arse again and again, he doesn't turn up, he (*Impersonates.*) 'can't cope, I just can't cope'. He complains about every single little thing we do and then he decides (*Impersonates again.*) 'hold the blue . . . at this stage . . . '

LOTI. Alright alright.

LAPO. Not alright! Lord, how can you do Genesis, from the celestial canopy above to the roiling waters of the Flood with no lapis, no azurite, no . . . *blue*?!

LOTI. Do you know what occurred to me?

LAPO. What??

LOTI. When we were doing the drunkenness of Noah.

LAPO. Yes??!

LOTI. And we've done Noah, right, lying there, ashamed of his nakedness in front of his daughter, right?

LAPO. There was plenty of blue when he was happily sploshing away on wet skim, wasn't there? Plenty of blue then.

LOTI. And Noah is all ashamed of his nakedness, and his sons come in to – like – cover him up and everything because they're embarrassed or whatever . . .

LAPO. What he means is that 'at this stage' he's used all his blue on a complete fiasco which we had to hack off and redo, and the Jesuits of San Giusto are quite sensibly refusing to cover his arse.

LOTI. What I want to know is: how come, when the sons of Noah come in to cover him up, like – in his embarrassment – how come we did *them* all naked too? Doesn't that kind of ruin the story?

LAPO. Oh marvellous, fucking marvellous. We spend two months redoing fourteen giornatas because Milly the master is out of his depth and uses up all his blue, and my boy is worried about the story being ruined. Listen, pal, get this into your head: they're all going to be naked on the ceiling from now on, alright? Every single, last, pissing, ancient progenitor of them. Noah, his sons, the prophets – Naked! All of the sybils, from the Delphic to the Eritrean – Naked! David! Solomon! Booz! Eliakim! Manasses! – Bare! When Mordecai, cousin of Esther punished Haman for usurping him and expelling the Jews from Persia? – He did it in the buff! Adam and Eve! – Even *after* the fall, when they're supposed to've covered themselves up – Naked! Jonah, Aminadab, Josephat, Jeremiah, Achim, Eliud, Daniel, Holofernes . . . Azor and Sadok – All of them stark-bollock, arse-bendingly, pillow-bitingly, buttock-tantalisingly nude! Because we are in the unwilling employ of an ugly little maggot of perversion called Michelangelo Buonnaroti, and the sphincter-mouth has run out of blue! At this stage.

Pause.

LOTI. I could always go down to the Raphael rooms and see if they've got any spare I could nick. My mate Briacci said Raphael has ordered so much stuff, he doesn't know what he's got.

LAPO. Oh brilliant. Well, why don't you do just that? And see if you can see your intensely spiritual meat-sack while you're down there and give her a bit more secret information.

LOTI. Naah. She wouldn't be down there! . . . Would she? And anyway, if she was, I'd just blank her. And I could see if they've got any wine. Eh? Would you like that, Laps? Some wine?

LAPO. Wine?

LOTI. Maybe it'd look a bit better pissed.

LAPO. Listen, pal, I fresco. Alright? I don't do anything else. I've been doing it since I was nine years old. I was on San Lorenzo. I was on San Ferdiano's in Lucca, mate. I met Pollaiolo. 'The Life of the Baptist'? I mixed pigment for that. I haven't got time for intense moments or spiritual moments 'like Plato says'. Alright? I don't go with women, I don't go with men. I don't get drunk, I fresco. And I send money back to my sons in Ferrara, the lazy bastards. And my poor mother. When I get paid, that is. And no matter how much money I send, I still cannot teach them wisdom, alright? I fresco and I cannot fresco without – fucking – blue.

LOTI (*nodding too much*). Right. Right.

LOTI *swallows his mouthful and gets up gingerly to go to the trap door from which they entered. He edges towards it. When he gets to the opening of the trap he looks down and gets vertigo. He edges slowly to the ladder and puts one toe on it, clutching the side. He is terrified.*

LAPO. Get down there!

LOTI. Couldn't I have a harness?

LAPO (*roars at him*). Aaargh!!

LOTI *disappears down the trap. LAPO threatens LOTI with a paint pot which is in his hand. He puts it down. After LOTI has gone, he returns to pick up the pot but accidentally kicks it while bending down to pick it up. It falls through the hole. Two to three seconds later we hear a bang and an 'Oi' from LOTI below. Then a further three seconds of clattering and its resounding echo. Then silence.*

LAPO *takes another piece of charcoal or pigment and brush, and returns to the wall. He takes a few deep breaths before starting to draw on the wall, joining up the dots he previously blew or patted on in charcoal dust. As the outline of the drawing emerges, he becomes more focused, his breathing deeper and steadier. He stands back every now and then to get a longer view. Subliminally at first, a piece of music has begun and continues to creep up on us – like the opening of Gorecki's 'Sorrowful Songs'. LAPO's concentration is now total and a large image is taking shape on the back wall. It is the head, shoulders and left hand of the prophet Isiah. A miracle is happening.*

After a while, we become aware of the clattering and panting of LOTI who is climbing back up the ladder to the trap entrance. LAPO stops momentarily, to acknowledge this, but continues to draw in ever-increasing sweeping motions. It is almost as if he is in a slow-motion combat with the back wall. It takes LOTI quite a while to get to the top and appear at the trap. When, eventually, he arrives, he is covered in paint from the pigmentation pot knocked onto his head on the way down. He looks very silly now. He stands for a moment, clutching the top of the ladder, completely out of breath. LAPO continues to draw.

LAPO. You look ridiculous.

LOTI. You should see the Pope.

LOTI *has obviously come back up the ladder too fast. He is breathless and is not carrying any wine or fresh pigments from the Raphael rooms.*

No, I mean . . . you should see the Pope. He's a goner, Lapo. Malaria . . .

LAPO (*irritated*). Now what?!

LOTI. . . . They've taken him to Castel St Angelo . . . They've called in Francesco Alidosi to issue last rites . . .

LAPO. What, again? How many lives does this pope have?

LOTI. The French have taken Brescia, and they're bringing Briacci's canon with them to fire at the Pope.

LAPO. It's the French this time, is it?

LOTI. It's dangerous out there! The old women are building a barricade on the Via Vittorio! There's no one in charge, Lapo. Pack up your things. We . . . gotta get out of here!

LAPO *stops drawing.*

LAPO. Are you sure?

LOTI. Yes! Come on!

LAPO. I was just . . . The temperature is just right . . . What about your friends downstairs?

LOTI (*gathering up his own things*). There's no one around down there. The place is empty, Lapo. There's only us here! Everyone's gone. We got to get out of here. Fast!

LAPO. But . . . what about the ceiling?

LOTI. What ceiling? There might not even be a chapel by tomorrow! Oh yeah. And Milly's run away to Florence!

LAPO. What?

LOTI. Yeah, he went yesterday evening. Come on.

LAPO *starts to pack up his things too.*

LAPO. So he just buggered off, did he, without telling us? Nice.

LOTI. Come on! Let's go!

LAPO. Yeah yeah. Alright, alright . . . Alright!

LOTI *heads for the trap, followed by* LAPO *with a quickly assembled bag of things.* LOTI *disappears down the ladder. On his way out,* LAPO *takes a last look at the drawing on the wall and notices an unfinished line which could be improved. He cannot help himself. He dumps his things on the floor and, picking up a piece of charcoal or a brush from the floor, goes back to the wall to quickly draw a correction. He stands back to look. There is another shout from* LOTI, *below.* LAPO *exits down the trap, after one last look at his work.*

End of Act One.

ACT TWO

Scene One

One year later.

A rough curtain has been drawn across the back of the platform, covering the plaster wall, but leaving enough space in front of it for a forestage. This is the Canzone stage of an artist's tavern in Padua.

LOTI puts his head out awkwardly through the centre parting of the curtain and then disappears. His head returns wearing a crap mitre which he has trouble keeping on as he walks through the curtains onto the forestage. He is uncomfortable and self-conscious. The following text is performed by LOTI and then LAPO as if it were a double-act show which they have devised. Some of it may be sung, or at least have musical accompaniment. LAPO is awkward, though more pissed off than self-conscious at having to perform their piece. LOTI is a keen, if wooden performer.

LOTI.
   I am the Pope – a big one too
   So I need a sprauntsy tomb
   With massive marble knobs on
   And frescoes in my room.

   For my grave I need a sculptor
   For my bedrooms, something nice
   I need the best at my request
   The good will not suffice.

LAPO enters wearing a silly red and gold Florentine jacket.

   Oh, and also there's a ceiling job
   Which I forgot to mention
   It's worth a few to an artist who
   Is thinking of his pension.

LAPO.

    Now I am just a sculptor
    Who prefers to work alone
    I want to carve that tomb so much
    I've even bought the stone.

    I'd like to try the sarcophagi
    With statues twelve feet tall
    Although I quite like fresco
    I wouldn't want it on my wall.

LOTI.

    Stop dithering, you Florentine
    D'you know with whom you're dealing?
    If you're that good I think you should
    Put pictures on my ceiling.

LAPO.

    I didn't ask for that holy task
    I begged to be released
    But before I could go I'd have to show
    The Pope a masterpiece!!

BOTH.

    Before you ask, the artist's task is tortuous and lengthy
    In calmer states he fondly waits for some artistic frenzy
    On wall or frame it's all the same from Roma to Firenze
    You bust your arse to ply your art and try 'n' surpass all envy.

LOTI (*coming out of his Pope character*).

    Thank you, thank you, thank you
    For your attention and your money
    We can't tell you how happy we are
    To be here in your Canzone.

    You're such a lovely audience
    He's Lapo, I am Loti
    We're here to tell what happened
    'Twixt the Pope and Buonnaroti.

LAPO (*no longer as Michelangelo*).

    For a few ducats, us hungry prats
    Will re-enact our story

It's full of grief and no relief
And someone else's glory.

Yes! We're here to celebrate
The great Michelangeloni
Who left his crew with nothing to do
But sing in the Canzone.

LOTI.

Yes! When the French had all departed
And the Pope's disease had passed
We hurried back to save our jobs
But were kicked out on our arse.

LAPO.

It's not for mess or being late
Or even for bad plaster
Our pointless end came cos my friend
Impersonates the master.

He swanned around in fancy gear
And since we were not paid
He figured, as the master
He might at least get laid.

After his little shenanigan
No one was surprised
To see our stuff on Raphael's wall
And the master plagiarised.

LOTI.

But it's not just us who suffered
At the master's selfish hand
It was all the noble artists
Who signed up for that band.

When the Pope was feeling better
And had made his peace with France

LAPO.

Our master fired everyone
And invested his advance.

He'd sacked his best, then sacked the rest
Was ordered back to Rome

LOTI.

And climbing those three hundred steps
He carried on alone.

In the last few months he painted
What'd take ten artisans a year
And even though he's not quite done
The Pope is off to see 'er.

LAPO.

Oh, lucky Pope to gaze at last
On what our master did!

LOTI.

Oh, lucky Michelangelo!
To finally get rid!

LAPO (*a moment of gravity*).

We never got paid for the work we'd done
Never even got respect
To play one's part in a master's art
Whole families are wrecked.

We gave our lives, our sons' and wives'
Our knowledge and our game
And now we'll die in shallow graves
Which bear our master's name.

LOTI (*back as Pope*).

Being Pope's not easy
Cos you have to stay alive
When others might have given up
I shout 'I will survive!'

My constitution's legendary
While lesser men have died
From cannonballs and malaria
I took them in my stride.

I kept the French from Italy
The warring dukes apart
And booked my ticket heavenwards
By subsidising Art.

(*Points at* LAPO.) Get on with it, you Artist!
Just do as you are told
And when the ceiling's finished
Cover it in gold!

LAPO.

Before you ask, the artist's task is tortuous and lengthy
In calmer states he fondly waits for some artistic frenzy
On wall or frame it's all the same from Roma to Firenze
You bust your arse to ply your art and try 'n' surpass all envy.

BOTH.

The master only worked in stone until in fifteen ten he
Began at last to do the task that would surpass all envy
He hid the cash in a church's stash but then he fired his
    men; he –
Bust his arse to ply his art to try 'n' surpass all envy.

*They exit clumsily, in a dustman dance. LOTI, very pleased
to accept applause; LAPO, surprised and dismissive of it.*

Scene Two

*The scaffolding platform once more. In the distance we can
hear the chanting of monks and its echo. The back wall is
blank once more with a new skim coat of plaster on it. Where
the upstage-right hole in the floor was, is a neater opening
next to a crane with a pulley-wheel made of wood, with its
ropes dangling down to the floor of the chapel below. A large,
empty canvas bag is suspended just below the floor level of the
trap. Lying on the floor around the crane-pulley are various
other canvas bags, boxes and pots – some full, some empty.*

*It is late afternoon – early evening, and the sun, low in the sky,
is sending strong beams of light across the platform. From
down below, we hear a massive door being pulled shut and
bolted. The chanting of the monks becomes fainter and
eventually disappears.*

*After a pause, one of the canvas bags moves a little, then stops.
It moves again.*

LAPO (*from inside the bag*). Loti? Are you there, Loti?

The bag stirs again and after a struggle with the bindings,
LAPO *thrusts his head out of the top.*

Loti? Did you make it?

LAPO *gets out of the bag. He is wearing a monk's habit.*
He looks off left and right to check that he is alone, then
starts to search among the other bags and boxes,
whispering for LOTI. *He goes to the upstage-right hole,*
where the pulley is, and whispers at first, then louder –
down the hole. We hear his echo.

Loteeeee! Have you let me down? Again?

He pulls one of the pulley ropes and the attached canvas
bag comes into view. The bag is obviously full of building
debris, not LOTI. *He lets go of the bag and it whizzes to the*
ground below. We hear it clatter to the bottom and echo.
The canvas counterweight bags come shooting back up and
almost attack LAPO. *He looks downstage and across the*
auditorium for LOTI.

It was a *simple* set of instructions. Do I have to do
everything for y–

He is stopped in his tracks by the sight of the almost-
finished ceiling out over the auditorium. He is shocked and
not a little bit humbled at what he sees. He looks all
around. This is not what he was expecting. There is a
muffled scream from somewhere on the platform behind
him. It snaps him out of his reverie.

LOTI (*from inside something*). Waaaah!

LAPO. Loti?

LAPO *goes to where the scream came from – a large*
packing case – and rips off the side to reveal LOTI *curled*
up and clutching an empty bottle. LOTI *is wearing a very*
ill-fitting monk's habit.

LOTI. Are we there yet? I fell asleep.

LAPO (*whispering*). Get up!

LOTI (*still in his packing case*). Is it safe, Lapo? Have they all gone?

LAPO (*over his shoulder*). Get up, you amphibian!

LAPO takes off his monk's habit and throws it down near the sack in which he was hiding. Underneath it, he is no longer covered in plaster and paint, but is dressed very simply and shabbily. It is some months since he has worked.

LOTI (*still in his packing case*). Do you ever get that thing when you wake up and you don't know who you are? I mean, not just where you are, or what day it is – but actually who you are. *Whether* you are, even.

LAPO. You're a drunk. That's who you are.

LOTI. Oh yes. I know that. I'm aware of that. I couldn't wake up forgetting that – believe me. No, I mean, I am Lodovico del Buono, right? But sometimes all I am aware of when I wake up is that there is pain in the world. Or my knee, at any rate. Everything else is questionable. And sometimes I don't even know that. It's quite alarming.

LAPO. Have you finished *all* the wine then?

LOTI (*rummaging in his box and fetching things out*). No, there's another bottle and . . . some cheese . . . and . . . the bread . . . (*He has obviously been sitting on the bread*) . . . sorry . . . And this.

He produces a small flask from about his person and takes a sip from it. Without turning round, LAPO puts out his hand for a swig. LOTI passes it to him and notices the crane-pulley and all the other new equipment.

Wow!

(*Looking at the smooth edges of the hole in the platform and the crane-pulley.*) Nice. Wish we'd had one of these.

LOTI fiddles with the pulley, it clanks.

LAPO. Sssshhhh!

LAPO gazes up at the ceiling again, but eventually his body cannot take the strain and he breaks back upstage.

LOTI. Come on. Let's eat first and then we can look at it.

> LOTI *takes off his monk's habit and gets out the bread, cheese and wine and makes a sort of picnic-spread by the boxes. LAPO finds it hard to take his eyes from the ceiling. Even while eating. But, as before, he does not really eat. He takes a couple of mouthfuls half-heartedly through the following dialogue. LOTI, on the other hand, only looks up at the ceiling when the food is laid out and he is sitting comfortably, eating. LOTI is childishly meticulous about sharing out exactly equal portions of everything. They look at the ceiling and eat. They look at one section for a few seconds, then, in unison, they choose different positions and look at another. At one point LOTI touches LAPO's arm and points to a bit he's spotted. LAPO nods sullenly.*

What's the Pope going to think about that bit?

LAPO. He'll regret telling the master that he could paint whatever he chose, that's what.

> *Pause while LOTI eats, and they look at the ceiling.*

LOTI. Well. It's come on a bit, hasn't it?

LAPO. Yup. Still not finished, though. Milly's got to show it to the Pope tomorrow whether it's ready or not. Pope got tired of waiting.

LOTI. Exciting, isn't it?

LAPO. What?

LOTI. Getting to see it before the Pope even. Before anyone.

LAPO. I told you.

LOTI. You told me how we were going to get ourselves up here. But you never said how we were going to get out again. You do have a plan for that. Don't you, Lapo?

LAPO. How long did it take you to become a silversmith, Loti?

LOTI. Couple of years – but I never really finished. My chest, you know – but yeah, couple, three.

LAPO. Lucky you met me, eh?

LOTI. Yeah, 'course. I mean, I could never have got here otherwise, could I? I'd be out of a job, wouldn't I?

LAPO. You are out of a job.

LOTI. Oh yes. I am out of a job. But you know what I mean. Knowing fresco.

LAPO. Exactly. A year or two drawing on small panels, six years cooking lime and applying plaster. Embossing it, scraping it, gilding it. Not for wimps, this game.

LOTI. Rough casting it.

LAPO. Another six learning to paint on it. It's a joke really, isn't it?

LOTI. Yeah, sod that. Easier to be an architect, they can just do what they like.

LAPO. Yeah. And half the buildings fall down. Naah. Fresco is definitely the toughest.

LOTI. So, what do we think of it, Lapo? Work of a genius? Or . . . ?

LAPO. Genius? What's that? Just someone born with the right personal shortcomings at the right time. It's about teamwork. We're all laced together, aren't we? Like the pontarolos who made this scaffold? – one wrong step from one of them and they're all a mess on the floor. We are all interdependent. If the ancients hadn't been arsing around with poisonous limecast in the first place, then no one would have worked out how to cover it in images, would they?

LOTI. Yeah. Alright, alright.

LAPO. If Cimabue hadn't picked up on it, even Leonardo'd be doing pub theatre. It's a dialogue, like Plato. If Socrates hadn't liked a bit of a conversation what could Plato have written?

LOTI. You know, Raphael added a picture of the master as an ugly runt to that School of Athens just to wind him up?

LAPO. Yeah, exactly, it's like we're all woven together into a seam.

LOTI. I know what you mean. It's like, two people can have the same idea at the same moment. I've often thought that.

LAPO. I was just going to say that. And yet, for some reason, only one of them gets to sign it off. All of our work – his name.

LOTI. That's quite handy too, though, isn't it? Because if it's a really bad idea then at least one of you doesn't get punished. Mind you, when I got the sack, Milly fired you as well. Sorry about that.

LAPO. Guilty by association. But no one ever gets rich by association, do they?

LOTI. No. I suppose not. Anyway, Milly fired everyone in the end.

LAPO. Yes. All those little personal masterpieces up there to glorify the great Buonarroti. It's robbery really, isn't it? Unethical acquisition. The misappropriation of our souls.

LOTI. Well, it's up there now and I think it's looking pretty fine – all in all.

LAPO. And don't you mind that what was yours is now his?

LOTI. No, I mean, I think it's more important to look at the thing as a whole, you know – than like, think of it as just all the separate bits put together.

LAPO. So why are you here?

LOTI. Cos you and me were crap as pub entertainers and you said it would be easy as pox to sneak in here and be the first to see it. Before the Pope even.

LAPO. No, dish-wipe. I mean, what's the point of making this? Why were you with me?

LOTI. Oh, I see. Well, originally because I got fired from Bertoldo the silversmith's and there wasn't much else on. You know already.

LAPO. But why this? Why particularly here?

LOTI. Well, it's good to be part of something important, I
suppose. When I was on that rough-coat-plastering job on
the walls of San Torrino in Pisa, with Sodoma – they were
crap, they were. We had to abandon them after thirteen
months cos it looked like the whole place was going to fall
apart anyway. And you really had to watch your arse with
that guy, I can tell you. Oh yes, missus. So, yes, it's nice to
feel that you're part of a big one – you know, a job like this,
it was exciting, wasn't it? I'm sorry I got us fired, Lapo, it's
my fault.

LAPO. No, what I meant was – what was in it for us?

LOTI. Well, everybody's heard of this one. Everybody's
waiting to see how it'll turn out. Who's going to win.

LAPO. Who's going to win?

LOTI. Yes, you know. Milly or the Pope. Raphael or Milly. The
Medici or the Republic – you know, it's exciting. Like when
you get to see a big massacre or a public execution, you
know. Fun.

LAPO. That is one way of going through life, I suppose.

LOTI. I saw the burning, you know. When I was a kid. I saw
them burning Savonorola. Must've been when I was
fourteen or something. It was fantastic. There were at least,
ooh, a thousand people there. That's when I made up my
mind, you know – to sort of, go for it – get famous,
whatever. Go to Bologna, come to Rome. Some people
reckoned he was already dead, though – by the time they lit
the pyre. I mean, there was no writhing agony or anything.
But anyway, it was still a hell of a show.

LAPO. So, you have no sense of duty, then? No . . . integrity?
No Devotion? Not even a scrap of Divine yearning in you?

LOTI. No. Not really, no. Do I have to?

LAPO. And doesn't it bother you that you can't really come up
with one, compelling reason to have been here? Other than
a desire to be 'part of something famous'?

LOTI. Oh, come on, Lapo, what does it matter *why* we do it? It only matters *that* we do it. We'll never know what God thinks of us; who he thinks is alright, who he's going to shit on. We do it, that's enough. If I'm mixing your pigments, or passing you the stylus, I'm not thinking 'why?' Like knowing which brush to pass when you snap your fingers. I haven't got time to think *'why?'* I just reach for the brush. I'm happy then and God leaves me alone when He knows I'm happy. It's one less thing for Him to worry about.

LAPO. And when you arrive at Heaven's Gate, and you're in the queue and there's Milly ahead of you and St Peter says 'Well done, Milly; well done, old girl, we love your work. We appreciate the gifts you bring. And despite being the one so overly rewarded already on earth, we're going to reward you again now you're here. You can come in right now. Go up the stairs and turn left. Your throne is up there waiting. Follow the golden light, my old mucker. Right, you others! You oiks! Get back down there for a few more million years of Purgatory! Go on the lot of you! Get out of my sight!' What are you going to do then? You going to be happy then? What you going to say then?

LOTI. Well, I don't know if it'll be quite like that. Maybe I will be happy then too. I don't know.

LAPO. I'll tell you what you're going to say, 'Just a minute!' You're going to say, 'I did some of that.' You're going to say, 'Let me in too. Maybe not upstairs with my own throne and everything, but I deserve to come in at least and hang about with a few cardinals on the ground floor, surely?'

LOTI. Yeah, maybe I'll regret it then. I don't know. Maybe I'll have to repent for a bit. Ages. Who knows what God is trying to tell us?

LAPO. 'Milly's not that good!' You'll say. 'She fucked up Noah and the Flood completely. We had to fix it for her!' You'll say, 'There was fucking mildew on it! Mildew! Let me in.'

LOTI. Probably not such a good idea to shout at St Peter like that . . . And you might have to watch the swearing too.

LAPO. Yes yes, obviously. But you know what I fucking mean.
It's just not . . . it's not right, it's not . . . sometimes when I
draw, it's as if God is in my breath. It's as if my heart beats
to a rhythm outside of me. I am not breathing, I am, I am . . .
being breathed. Doesn't happen every time. But it is more
pleasant to feel this than anything. Than, than eating a
peach. Than the act of love. It is the reason I am without my
sons. I could have stayed in Ferrara and made bricks. Their
mother would have been happier. My mother would have
been spared her struggle. Of course I send money back
when I can. When I get paid. But it is never enough. My
sons do not respect me. (*He looks out at the opposite wall,
stage right.*) You see that buttock there?

LOTI. Which one?

LAPO. There, beyond Ezekiel.

LOTI. What – the cherub or Eve?

LAPO. Naoo. Not Eve, you melon head. Not the cherub. The
baby boy beyond Ezekiel.

LOTI. What – the one with the oak leaves?

LAPO. No. Ezekiel not Ezekias. Beyond Ezekiel.

LOTI. Oh. Erm. I don't know. I don't know who they all are.
Ezekiel – Ezekiarse. Please, Lapo.

LAPO *takes his arm and points so that* LOTI *will see.*

LAPO. There. That buttock.

LOTI *still doesn't get it.*

Terra rosa three and bianca with seven parts ochre.

LOTI. Oh! Yeah! That one.

LAPO. I did that.

LOTI. Did we?

LAPO. Yes. And that nose.

LAPO *walks* LOTI *to the other side of the stage.*

LOTI. What – Noah's nose?

LAPO. No, we did Noah's hand, remember?

LOTI. Right.

LAPO. Zorobabel's nose.

LOTI *is none the wiser.*

The one with the big tits.

LOTI. Oh, that one. (*Now he knows exactly where to look.*)

LAPO. And the toes of the sybil. And . . . and the entire story of the expulsion of Helidorus.

LOTI. Did we do that entire story? Blimey!

LAPO. Actually, that's just on that small medallion over there.

LOTI. Oh. Right.

LAPO. We did Noah's hand, Zorobabel's nose, the toes of the sybil, a small medallion and a buttock.

LOTI. Not bad.

LAPO. And that's apart from all the ariccio rough-coat from there to there – (*He indicates.*) and all the intonacco skim-coat from there . . . to there. And the hacking back of Noah's Flood and doing it again to save his arse.

LOTI. And preparing the colours and spolvero and bunging up all the cartoons. Before we got fired that is. I liked that bit.

LAPO. Yes. We taught him how to mix, how to transfer, how to plan a giornata.

LOTI. Doesn't look like he's got the hang of that yet. (*He is at the wall.*) Look, there's a whole giornata here with nothing on it. This'll be totally dry before morning.

LAPO. A hand, a nose, a buttock and some toes.

LOTI. And a medallion.

LAPO. Mmmm. And a medallion.

LAPO *goes back to his canvas bag and reaches inside it. After rummaging around he pulls out a small cloth bag which he dumps on the floor. From its ominous jangle we can tell it contains metal tools – such as a hammer and chisels.*

LOTI. Well, I think it's fantastic. I mean, the overall effect. . . you have to admit it's pretty impressive . . . well, I've never seen anything like it . . . I shouldn't think anyone has. (*He looks directly above them.*) And he's done it incredibly quickly if you think about it. I mean, all this. God knows how he got all that done in the time. Amazing really.

LOTI continues to look directly above them. The sun has shifted and the beam of light is now at a different angle. From his body language we see that he has noticed something unusual. He pursues what he has found across the top of the theatre, looking directly above his head and walking a few steps like a puppet.

Lapo?

But LAPO is in his own thoughts.

Lapo? Look at this! And there!

LAPO. A medallion. A hand. A buttock. Nose and toes.

LAPO is getting out a mallet and chisels from his cloth bag of tools. He tests the chisels for sharpness. LOTI is getting excited.

LOTI. Lapo! Come and look! He's . . . I don't know how he could have done that. The whole of that bit, with the big man in the pink nightie. There's no spolvero marks! Look! And there! And there! Nothing at all. And . . . wow! Look at that! It's like you're looking right up his arse! How the fuck did he paint that? Straight onto the ceiling? Wow, Lapo! Come and look!

LAPO has chosen his tools. He has a grim expression on his face. While LOTI is enraptured by the ceiling, LAPO exits stage right, carrying with him his mallet and a quiver of chisels. Left alone, LOTI is still gazing up at God's creation.

I don't believe it, Lapo. He must have put that whole section there straight onto the ceiling! No spolvero, Lapo.

Nothing. And all in one giornata. It's not possible! And there too! Bloody hell! What about that?!

LOTI *is too engrossed to bother with his fear of heights now.*

Waaooow! (*He falls silent in awe. Then again.*) Waaaooooww!

From far away offstage left we hear the tapping of a chisel and its echo.

Lapo? (*Coming back to earth.*) Lapo?

Realising he is alone, and hearing the chisel tapping, LOTI rushes offstage-left, shouting after LAPO.

Lapooo!

We hear LOTI's footsteps and their echo. We hear shouting and arguing and then a fight. Because of the enormous echo it is difficult to make out exactly what they are saying, but odd words such as 'Get off me! . . . ' and 'Buttock – ock – ock' and 'That is my medallion . . . ' come back to us. After the sounds of a scuffle, we hear a short scream from LOTI and the clatter of a mallet and chisel bouncing down through the scaffold and ladders and hitting the floor below. There is a moment's silence after the echo dies away before we hear LAPO speak.

LAPO (*offstage*). Loti? . . . Loti?

LOTI (*offstage*). Aaaah! Over here!

LAPO (*offstage*). Loti? What are you doing there?

LOTI (*straining, offstage*). What . . . does it look like?

LAPO (*offstage*). It looks like a chicken on a clothes line.

LOTI (*in pain, offstage*). Aaah!

LAPO (*offstage*). Hang on! Hang on!

LOTI (*offstage*). I am . . . hanging!

LAPO (*offstage*). Put your foot out behind you . . . and there's a timber . . . no . . . other foot . . .

LOTI (*grunting, offstage*). Now what?

LAPO *enters and after checking through the trap upstage-right, he comes downstage to where there is a gap in the floorboards, crouches down and shouts through it.*

LAPO. Now, let go your left hand, Loti, let go your left hand . . . and . . . Loti? . . . Loti? . . . Where are you, Loti? . . . Oh Lord! . . . What have I done? . . . Loti-Loti-Loti!!

Through the trap, a hand appears dramatically. Then another. Then a foot and an ankle. Then a leg. LOTI *is trying to climb up back onto the stage from below. He makes a bad job of it and slips back down. Eventually, with his cheek flattened to the floor and his leg in the air, he gets stuck.* LAPO *is still downstage looking through the floorboard.*

LOTI. Well, help me up, Laps, you shag brain.

During the following dialogue, LAPO *goes to help him up and pulls on the protruding leg.* LOTI *is being deliberately awkward. They succeed and fall backwards onto the stage.* LAPO *is not amused. They are both out of breath.*

LAPO. You shouldn't have done that. You should not have done that. That was really stupid.

LOTI. And you shouldn't even've *thought* of doing *that*!

LAPO. Apart from anything else, you gave me a fright. I thought you were gone.

LOTI. Well, there was no need to shove me like that! You know how big my feet are.

LAPO. Well, you jumped on my back.

LOTI. Jumped? I did not jump! I tried with reasonable force to restrain you.

LAPO. Huh.

LOTI. I just couldn't let you do that, Lapo. Like you said, we *make* fresco. We don't chop bits off fresco just because the master is a bit of an arse when it comes to credit. And money. And respect.

LAPO. How do you think I would have got through the rest of my life with that as a memory? How many confessions would have sufficed?

LOTI. But Lapo, look. Look at the ceiling. Look what he's done.

LAPO. I know what he's done.

Now that he is back on the platform, LOTI *grabs* LAPO*'s head and holds it up to the ceiling. He points it in various directions.*

LOTI. Look. No spolvero. Just onto the ceiling. Freehand. And all in one giornata! And there.

LAPO *resists, but is held by* LOTI *still.*

Look, Lapo, do you see?

LAPO. I see. I see.

LOTI. And there, amazing.

LAPO. I see.

LOTI. Genius, eh? God and His miracles, Milly and his.

LAPO (*looking unassisted now*). I see it. Alright?

LOTI. And on the eighth day he created a ceiling, eh? Well, it probably took him a little bit more than eight days.

LAPO. I am aware of the achievement.

LOTI. Ooooh, it sort of swirls you round, doesn't it, Lapo? Cor! Look at the thighs on that bloke with the fish, Lapo!

LOTI *grabs* LAPO *again to make him look. In a frenzied struggle,* LAPO *pushes* LOTI *onto the floor and pins him down.*

LAPO. Shut up! Just shut up!

LOTI. But look at the . . .

LAPO. Shut up, you Florentine!!

LOTI. Actually, I'm originally from Pisa. I only went to Florence when I was six.

LAPO *stays holding* LOTI *down to the floor in an arm-lock.*

I don't have to stay, you know! I don't have to stay around with you! Even if we had something to paint. I could leave. Is that what you want?

Pause. They stay motionless for a moment or two.

I don't know why you can't just enjoy what you got.

LAPO *lets go of* LOTI, *roughly, and stalks away.*

(*Getting up.*) I used to really think you were the best, you know. That you knew everything.

LAPO. Yeah, well, that was stupid because I know nothing. I am nothing. What am I? Just a plasterer. Who am I? Just a splodge.

LOTI. If you want to create anything, you have to forget who you are. You said that, master.

LAPO. Huh. Well, I don't know what I'm talking about most of the time. You're a fool for listening.

LOTI. No, you were right. You have to forget it. Whoever you are. And it must be the same for Milly too. He didn't want this job.

LAPO. No, it's not! No! It's not the same. At least for him the sacrifices are worth it! I gave up just as much as him, suffered just as much, to produce what . . . ? At least Milly has the compensation of . . . of that. (*He indicates the ceiling.*)

LOTI. Just because Milly did something great, doesn't immediately make you shit . . .

LAPO (*broken*). I just . . . keep . . . getting in my own way! I just want to lose this small . . . stuffy . . . overcoat – that is me!!

LOTI. But . . . you are Lapo d'Antonio. No point in regretting that.

LAPO. Why didn't he take us with him, Loti? Why did he leave us behind?

LOTI. He didn't leave us behind, he fired us! But the point is, we're still up there, aren't we? He's taken us with him whether he likes it or not. Even if it is just some toes and a buttock and half a medallion.

LAPO. I am a mean, bitter, little man, Loti. That's who I am.

LOTI. But that ceiling doesn't give a toss who you are, Lapo. Nor who Milly is neither.

The sun is about to set. It is dusk. The beam of light from the window is now almost horizontal and is shining directly onto the back wall.

Anyway, I reckon you should be proud. Of Milly, I mean. Of what he's done with our work. You think he could've done any of that without you teaching him where to start . . .

LAPO. Teacher? Huh. And what have I taught you, eh?

LOTI. Yeah . . . but don't give up now . . . you can't just give up! . . . What am I supposed to do if you give up? . . . Tell me what to do next . . . Lapo? . . . master? . . .

LOTI *turns in desperation to look at the blank wall and ceiling behind him.*

(*To the wall.*) And you can shut up! All blank and empty! And damp and . . . and ready! And staring at us – waiting to be covered . . . (*He interrupts himself, noticing something on the ceiling above them.*) Oh my . . . Mother of . . . Christ! Lapo! Look! He's put your face on one of those angels in that cloud!

LAPO (*looking up sharply*). Which one?!

LOTI. Ha ha! Fooled you! Fooled you! Got you! (LOTI *runs on the spot with glee.*) You are the fool! You are the master's tool!

LAPO (*smiling despite himself*). No, I'm not . . . Anyway, it looks more like your arse than my face.

LOTI. Actually, if it wasn't a blasphemy, I'd say that was God's arse up there.

LOTI *has succeeded in getting* LAPO *to look up at the ceiling again. They both stop and stare up at it for a moment. They sigh.*

LAPO (*in awe*). Immortal, eh? The whole fucking story, eh? The whole struggle to be immortal through beauty.

LOTI. Yeah. Two lovely, beautiful, immortal buttocks.

LAPO. Not entirely what I meant, but . . . immortal through a buttock . . . yeah.

Pause.

So . . . what do you reckon he'll be putting in this last bit? Another sybil? (LAPO *looks across the auditorium to the other wall of the chapel to compare the shape in the plaster behind him.*) . . . sitting on a dais . . . looking at a book . . . what d'you reckon would've been our contribution to that?

LOTI. We'd've done his dais for him and he could bung his sybil on top . . .

LAPO. So – the corner of the pilaster, the dais, the edging of the lunette maybe . . .

LOTI. . . . and maybe a couple of roseate folds along the bottom here? . . . a couple of roseate folds by the edge of the pillar? . . . Master? . . .

LAPO. No. Jeremiah over there is already roseate – this one'd have to be verdant. Or citrine. Anyhow, the folds are part of the sybil so forget the folds, he can worry about the folds . . .

LOTI. I've forgotten them already . . . and a few more oak leaves there . . .

LAPO. . . . and there . . . a suggestion of cherubs, maybe . . .

LOTI. Oh yeah, just a hint of cherubs . . .

LAPO. . . . fiddling with each other or whatever, on a small pillar there . . . hmmm.

Pause while they both consider the wall and ceiling.

LOTI. We don't actually have a cartoon to transfer, master. So we'd have to do it Milly's way. Transfer straight on the ceiling from our stunted imaginations. No spolvero . . .

LAPO *looks at* LOTI, *impressed by his protégé.*

LAPO. Clear up that mess over there.

LOTI. Yes, master.

LAPO. And is there enough water to wash the brushes out properly afterwards?

LOTI (*checking*). Erm . . . yes.

They start a 'preparation to work' routine similar to the one in Act One, chucking things across at each other.

LAPO. And what have we got?

LOTI (*looking among the boxes*). Most of what we'll need. We can mix up another ochre with what's left here. Better make it a bit good, eh? Milly showing it to Julius tomorrow, eh? What about that! Woooaarr! This is the big one!

LOTI looks up to see that LAPO is distracted at the surface of the wall, testing its dampness as he did in Act One. LOTI happily returns to sorting out the pigments.

LOTI starts to sing the first line of a song which they will continue to sing throughout the next sequence in which the pigments are prepared.

There once was a whore from old Milan
Who smelt like skanky old frying pan
She had fish scales all down her back . . .

LAPO (*joining in*).
And a haddock's fin sticking out of her crack.

They sing the song neither with gusto nor diffidence, but purely as a rhythmical tool to help them work.

LOTI. Oh yes, master. You have to be hard to fresco, I know. Not everyone can do it. Old Puccio Cappanna died doing it, and he had shoulders like an ox. It's pretty chilly, and the wind can blow right up your apron.

LAPO. I know, I know. And it ruins your eyesight. (*In his Michelangelo impersonation.*) 'Do you know, after doing this, my neck is going to be permanently in this position? It is. (*He demonstrates.*) If I want to eat, I have to sit on the floor and get someone to scrape the food off the edge of the table so it falls down my throat. Falls.'

LOTI. Yeah. Must be hard just being Milly. Poor old love.

LOTI goes to the pots and bags and produces five brushes which he presents to LAPO, fan like, over his elbow. LAPO considers the brushes and takes two from LOTI.

BOTH. And every boy and every man
   All of the people who sampled her fish
   Her limpets, crabs and whelks and clams
   They soon discovered were starting to itch.

   Limpets, muscles, whelks and clams
   She cockled their cockles and winkled their hams
   Limpets, crabs and whelks and clams
   She cockled their cocks and she winkled their hams.

While LAPO *works over by the back wall,* LOTI *finishes clearing up the mess.* LAPO *begins to sketch out a small section of the wall between the two lunettes. He draws the shapes of the dais in the area beneath the feet of the Libyan sybil. After a while,* LOTI *looks over to* LAPO.

LOTI. I've done you another ochre here. You should have everything you need?

   LAPO *is engrossed and ignores him.*

   Lapo? You got everything you need? Anything more I can do?

   LAPO *gives a cursory wave over his shoulder without looking round, as if to say 'let me concentrate'.* LOTI *looks at him for a few seconds and then makes the decision to leave.*

   Well, I'll be off then. Tara.

   LOTI *gets his bag and finds the flask. It is empty.* LOTI *peers down the trap, hesitantly. He returns stage left to get his monk's habit. Slinging that over his arm, he starts towards the ladder. Another thought occurs to him . . .*

   Let me know if you hear of any work . . .

   He starts down the ladder. When he is waist high in the trap, he pauses for a moment to contemplate the ceiling with satisfaction. He leaves, whistling. LAPO *has continued to work through all this. Now he hums to himself.*

LAPO.
   For breakfast she'd wolf down waffles and meat
   And at lunch a bunch of cheeses she'd eat

In the evenings she'd dine on a vegetable dish
But at night she'd be gobbling the old shell fish
Limpets, crabs and whelks and clams
She cockled their cockles and winkled their hams.

As LAPO *paints/draws, the rhythm of his singing/chanting
has been taken up, almost subliminally, by an ambient piece
of music which grows in volume and confidence over the
next sequence. The music should be inspirational and
repetitive, as if by Arvo Pärt, Terry Riley or Philip Glass,
and should have non-specific resonances of church choral
music. The sounds of angels.* LAPO *is breathing long and
slow now. He works, kneeling on the floor upstage-centre.
He should not appear to be rushing. Every now and then he
stands back to survey his work, or refill a jar, but this does
not halt his graceful rhythm.*

Above LAPO*'s head, on the major central portion of the
back wall, vast swathes of effervescent colour begin to
appear. Unseen by* LAPO, *the Libyan sibyl, in full glorious
yellow, is being painted as if by a giant magic hand on the
back wall/ceiling. Eventually* LAPO *is left in the shadows.
The actor playing* LAPO *gets up and puts his paint palette
to one side. Slowly, he makes his way around the stage,
blowing out candles. He takes off his apron and jacket and,
from a hook on one of the scaffolding ladders, he fetches a
red and gold jacket. Standing centrestage and facing
upstage, he puts this jacket on. He is no longer* LAPO, *but*
MICHELANGELO. *The music subsides to a sustained note
– we are now in a different time and place.*

*Slowly, out of darkness, a bare-headed man with a white
beard appears. As more of him becomes visible, we realise
that he is wearing the opulent white robes and jewellery of
the* POPE. *He is* JULIUS II, *the guv'nor. A* CARDINAL
*follows him, carrying his train. When the two of them have
finally arrived, the* CARDINAL *arranges the folds of the*
POPE*'s train and stands discreetly to the side.*

The POPE *looks around him and out into the auditorium.
He is surveying the finished ceiling. He takes two steps in
one direction and looks up for a while. Then two steps in*

another and looks up again. Occasionally the actor playing
LAPO, *now* MICHELANGELO, *indicates humbly with his*
arm where next the POPE *should look. Once or twice the*
POPE *nods to* MICHELANGELO, *but we cannot tell*
whether he approves or not.

With a wave of his white gloved finger, the POPE *beckons*
the CARDINAL *over to him. The* POPE *whispers*
something gently in the CARDINAL'*s ear. The* CARDINAL
nods, and speaks to MICHELANGELO.

CARDINAL. Erm . . . His Holiness would like to know if
there is to be more . . . gold.

MICHELANGELO *pauses for a moment and then shakes*
his head respectfully. The POPE *whispers once more in the*
CARDINAL'*s ear. The* CARDINAL *speaks in a calm and*
oily way, like a seasoned bureaucrat.

His Holiness suggests that when you do the secco – it might
afford you the opportunity then to include some . . . gold. To
make the whole thing . . . look . . . (*He looks to the* POPE
for approval.) . . . richer.

MICHELANGELO *again shakes his head. Sadly this time.*
The POPE *whispers again.*

If it is a question of budget . . .

MICHELANGELO *shakes his head.*

But there is to be a dry coat?

MICHELANGELO *shakes his head and looks to the floor.*
The CARDINAL *looks back to the* POPE *for permission.*
The POPE *nods and waves his hand to allow the*
CARDINAL *to speak 'off the record'. Even now, though, he*
speaks in the measured tones of one who has all the power.

You seem to have forgotten who you are, Michelangelo.
Forgotten where you are. Raphael has given His Holiness a
dry coat. And many saints. And glorious robes, and, and . . .
gold.

MICHELANGELO *shrugs like a teenager.*

(*Matter of fact.*) You are an insolent man, Michelangelo. An envious, insolent little man.

The POPE *raises his hand and nods the* CARDINAL *over to him. He whispers in his ear again. A slightly longer instruction this time.*

(*Speaking officially again.*) However . . . His Holiness is delighted with the overall effect – very impressive, never seen anything quite like it – and congratulates you on your four years of labour. You will receive a bonus of two thousand ducats which His Holiness knows you will have the wisdom to consider as a back payment for the marble you have already bought.

The POPE *nods to* MICHELANGELO – *the minimal gesture of threat needed from a very powerful man.* MICHELANGELO *acknowledges his nod. The* POPE *moves to leave.*

(*Smiling flatly.*) His Holiness bids you good day, and awaits some new sketches for His proposed sarcophagus with His customary fevered anticipation.

MICHELANGELO *kneels and kisses the* POPE's *outstretched hand. The* POPE, *assisted by the* CARDINAL *leaves. The music which had subsided, has crept back to an audible level. Slowly, and with difficulty,* MICHELANGELO *gets up and looks up at the ceiling. He is in quite a lot of pain, particularly in his knees and neck. He starts to leave through the trap. When he is waist-high on the stage, he takes one last look around at the walls and the ceiling, then out over the auditorium. The look on his face is neither one of triumph nor self-pity, but of resignation. Around him, a projection of the entire ceiling of the Sistine chapel is thrown onto the back wall, and if possible, a front stage gauze. As he turns to continue down the ladder, the light is gone.*

End.